presents

Maha Reiki®
Master Teacher
Manual

In Depth Reiki Training for Our Times

Donna Lambdin, Ph.D.
Ron Goodwin, Ph.D.

For online training webinar information,
please visit www.mahamethods.com

ACKNOWLEDGMENTS

Donna wishes to thank her guardian angel who is referred to as Grandmother, for reminding her of her sacred contract. This manual is in part the fulfillment of that contract. Donna also wants to express her gratitude to Lorrie Richmond for introducing her to Reiki and for being a wonderful friend and confidant. She also wants to thank her mentor Rosalie and her Reiki Master Teachers for their teachings, patience, and wisdom.

Many others have helped us on our journey, especially our Kundalini Yoga Instructor Shamsher.

Many thanks to David Elliot, Loni Wise, and Diana Daley for being the Reiki models. We thank Barbara DuBois for the cover design and page layout, along with her graphic illustrations; Lisa Lombardo for her cover and chapter header artwork.

The support and encouragement from our friends, students, clients, fellow Reiki Masters and Practitioners has been most helpful.

It was our privilege to meet an incredible artist while we were in Kona, Hawaii: Francene Hart. She has allowed us to use a few of her prints in our manual. For this we are forever grateful. Her website is *www.francenehart.com* and her mailing address is P.O. Box 900, Honaunau, HI 96726.

So much Love, Light, and Blessings to all on your Reiki journey.

Donna Lambdin and Ron Goodwin

DISCLAIMER

The purpose of this training manual is to assist Maha Reiki® Master Teachers and their students in understanding and learning Maha Reiki®. Maha Reiki® cannot be learned and practiced without receiving an attunement from a qualified Maha Reiki® Master Teacher.

The information in this manual is not medical advice and is not intended as a substitute for seeking medical attention.

TABLE OF CONTENTS

FOREWORD

The time is now!

In this current time of conscious development, fresh tools for teaching and learning are needed to assist in this journey. Many books have been written on Reiki, energetic, vibrational, and spiritual healing. Current mainstream magazines have recently published articles on a variety of alternative energetic healing methods, thus bringing the awareness of these methods to the public eye. The overview of these articles is sparking interest and awakening many people.

As individuals begin to awaken, many feel lost as to where to begin to find answers. The internet provides an immense amount of information, but where does a person go to find actual training? Hands on instruction is needed for Reiki and many other alternative healing methods. Many attunements and empowerments, unlocking the keys to raise vibrational consciousness, are passed on from teacher to student, in person.

Understanding, experiencing, and continuing guidance and support are important when a person is just beginning and continues to practice Reiki. Person to person contact fulfills this movement and growth. Becoming a Reiki Master Teacher or a Reiki Master Practitioner can be extremely supportive and comforting to yourself and others.

Maha Reiki® has developed over many years of practicing and teaching the Usui and Tibetan styles of Reiki. These teachings are the foundation of this practice. Maha is a Sanskrit word meaning "Great". New methods and ways of understanding the power of this amazing Reiki energy have grown and developed with daily practice and sessions with countless clients and students. "Do not minimize," these were the words spoken to me by Spirit. This guidance has assisted in my growth, continuing development, understanding, and teaching others advanced techniques with the Maha Reiki® energy.

This Maha Reiki® Master Teacher manual provides more advanced techniques and methods to empower and support the understanding and growth of your Reiki practice. This manual does not replace the need for the student to receive an in-person attunement from a qualified Maha Reiki® Master Teacher.

The time is now! Unlock your energetic, infinite potential!
Many blessings on your journey!

Donna Lambdin
Maha Reiki® Master Teacher

MAHA REIKI®
CODE OF ETHICS

The following are the basic operating principles of Maha Reiki® and our Code of Ethics.
All students, practitioners, and teachers should keep these principles in mind as they practice and teach Maha Reiki®.

1. Show gratitude for the gift of Reiki and for all fellow students, practitioners, and teachers, regardless of school or lineage.

2. Be honest, show respect, and have integrity in all you do.

3. Treat all information from clients, students, practitioners, and teachers in a confidential manner.

4. Recognize that Reiki works in conjunction with other forms of medical care. Never diagnose or prescribe medications. Refer clients other health care professionals when appropriate.

5. Always act in a professional manner and maintain a professional image.

6. Use common sense and seek the advice of experienced Maha Reiki® professionals when in doubt.

Welcome to Maha Reiki® Master Teacher Training!

Your journey has led you to this moment of moving forward into higher consciousness, higher vibration, and the ability to teach others!

Walking this journey with you is a great honor for me. My heart soars to greater heights as I witness the growth and understanding that you accomplish and allow to continue...Unfolding your talents, gifts, and connection to infinite energy.

The brilliant purity of your connection to Divine energy, highest light, which you continue to embrace and integrate into your daily practice, can lead you to places you cannot even imagine. For if you could imagine, you are putting limitations upon yourself.

Learning to trust, take each day as the gift it truly is. Flow without fear and worry. Fill with gratitude and honor. Let compassion be your guide, with every thought and action. Allow your spirit to soar to heights unimaginable, no limits, no barriers, only truth. Each day is new. Each day carries you closer to your highest consciousness and beyond!

Welcome to this class! Welcome to unconditional love that wraps you in a cocoon of divine, infinite light and possibilities...Namaste, Sat Nam.

Donna Lambdin
Maha Reiki® Master Teacher

Master Lineage

Dr. Mikao Usui

Kan'ichi Taketomi   Dr. Chujiro Hayashi

Kimiko
Koyama   Chiyoko Yamaguchi   Mrs. Hawayo Takata
Hiroshi Doi   Hyakuten Inamoto

Iris Ishikura   Iris Ishikura   Phyllis Lei Furumoto
Arthur Robertson   Arthur Robertson   Carol Farmer
Diane McCumber   Marlene Schilke   Leah Smith

Helen Haberlay

Mary Ellen Floyd

William Lee Rand
Colleen Benelli

Donna Lambdin

Ron Goodwin

THE FIVE PRECEPTS

Usui Sensei taught his students to place their hands together at their heart, morning and night, and repeat five precepts/principles. There are several similar interpretations of these precepts.
The following are the ones we are drawn to chant:

Just for today release anger

Just for today release worries

Earn your living honestly

Express gratitude

Be kind to every living thing

Repeating these precepts out loud, from your heart, can remind you, bring you joy in the moment, and carry you through your day with love!

Francene Hart

CHAKRA BALANCING MEDITATION

Sit comfortably with your spine as straight as possible, your feet flat on the floor or legs in easy pose.

Place your hands in Gassho, thumbs touching your heart.

Close your eyes. Take a few long slow deep breaths and slowly exhale out any tension or tightness. Relax the muscles around your ribs and any other area that may be constricting a full breath.

In your mind's eye, visualize and connect with the Earth Star, beneath your feet.

Feel your crown opening, connecting through your Crown and Star chakras to your highest mind, Cosmos, Divine infinite connection, brightest light from Source.

Slowly, starting from the Earth chakra, bring your long deep breath from the Earth through your entire body, to your light connection. Repeat three to five times.

When you feel relaxed, on your next breath up, chant LAM. Relax your chin. Open your mouth, do not clench your lips or teeth. Feel this long note vibrate your Root chakra for the entire breath. Repeat at least three times. Continue until you feel your Root chakra vibrating.

Once your Root chakra is vibrating, move up to your Sacral chakra.
Keep your chin relaxed and your spine straight. Feel the Earth chakra beneath your feet and your Crown and Star chakra opening to even greater amounts of Divine light flowing from the Cosmos.
Long deep breath, chant VAM. Feel your Sacral chakra vibrating with the long exhalation.
Repeat at least three times. Continue until you feel your Sacral chakra vibrating.
Now feel your Root and Sacral chakras vibrating together with the next breath.
Repeat this breath at least three times. Continue until you feel them spinning together.

Once you feel these two chakras spinning together, move up to your Solar Plexus chakra.
Keep your chin relaxed and your spine straight. Feel the Earth chakra beneath your feet and your Crown and Star chakra opening to even greater amounts of Divine light flowing from the Cosmos.
Long deep breath, chant RAM. Feel your Solar Plexus chakra vibrating with the long exhalation.
Repeat this breath at least three times. Continue until you feel your Solar Plexus chakra vibrating.
Now feel your Root, Sacral and Solar Plexus chakras vibrating together with the next breath.
Repeat this breath at least three times. Continue until you feel them spinning together.

Once you feel these three chakras spinning together, move up to your Heart chakra.
Keep your chin relaxed and your spine straight. Feel the Earth chakra beneath your feet and your Crown and Star chakra opening to even greater amounts of Divine light flowing from the Cosmos.
Long deep breath, chant YAM. Feel your Heart chakra vibrating with the long exhalation.

Repeat at least three times. Continue until you feel your Heart chakra vibrating. Feel the Heart growing, expanding with greater volumes of sound moving up from your lower chakras and more light flowing down from the Cosmos. Visualize your Heart as a glowing, growing, radiant expanding star.

Now feel your Root, Sacral, Solar Plexus, and Heart chakras vibrating together with the next breath. Repeat this breath at least three times. Continue until you feel them spinning together.

Once you feel these four chakras spinning together, move up to your Throat chakra.

Keep your chin relaxed and your spine straight. Feel the Earth chakra beneath your feet and your Crown and Star chakra opening to even greater amounts of Divine light flowing from the Cosmos.

Long deep breath, chant HAM. Feel your Throat chakra vibrating with the long exhalation. Feel the physical throat opening and expanding, allowing a greater volume of sound to vibrate through. Repeat at least three times. Continue until you feel your Throat chakra fully open and vibrating.

Now feel your Root, Sacral, Solar Plexus, Heart, and Throat chakras vibrating together with the next longer, deeper breath. Repeat this breath at least three times. Continue until you feel them spinning together.

Once you feel these five chakras spinning together, move up to your Third Eye chakra.

Keep your chin relaxed and your spine straight. Feel the Earth chakra beneath your feet and your Crown and Star chakra opening to even greater amounts of Divine light flowing from the Cosmos.

Long deep breath, chant OM. Feel your Third Eye chakra vibrating with the long exhalation. Feel the pineal and pituitary glands, behind your Third Eye, opening and expanding, allowing a greater volume of light and sound to vibrate through. Repeat at least three times. Continue until you feel your Third Eye chakra fully open and vibrating. Now feel your Root, Sacral, Solar Plexus, Heart, Throat, and Third Eye chakras vibrating together with the next longer, deeper breath. Repeat this breath at least three times. Continue until you feel them spinning together.

Once you feel these six chakras spinning together, move up to your Crown chakra.

Keep your chin relaxed and your spine straight. Feel the Earth chakra beneath your feet and your Crown and Star chakra opening to even greater amounts of Divine light flowing from the Cosmos.

Long deep breath, slowly exhale. Feel your Crown chakra vibrating and opening to even greater volumes of cosmic light flowing, with the long exhalation. Feel the pineal and pituitary glands, behind your Third Eye, opening and expanding more, allowing a greater volume of light to flow through. Repeat at least three times. Continue until you feel your Crown chakra fully open and vibrating.

Now feel your Root, Sacral, Solar Plexus, Heart, Throat, Third Eye, and Crown chakras vibrating and flowing together with the next longer, deeper breath. Repeat this breath at least three times. Continue until you feel them spinning together.

With your seven chakras spinning together, connected to your Earth and Star chakras, feel the movement and opening of your central channel. You now have a direct connection to infinite, Divine Light from Source and a grounding with the Mother Earth. You may experience a feeling of pure joy, euphoria, see colors, feel or see your Light Guides, or have many other amazing experiences.

Relax with your hands on your thighs, palms facing up in the receiving gesture, mudra.

Being connected and in balance is an opportune time to enjoy being completely relaxed, ask for guidance, release emotions or trauma, journey, etc, or just "BE."

SPINNING CHAKRAS

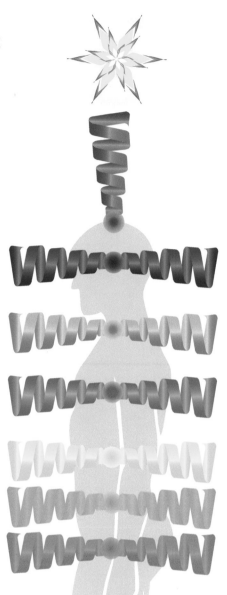

AURIC FIELD LAYERS

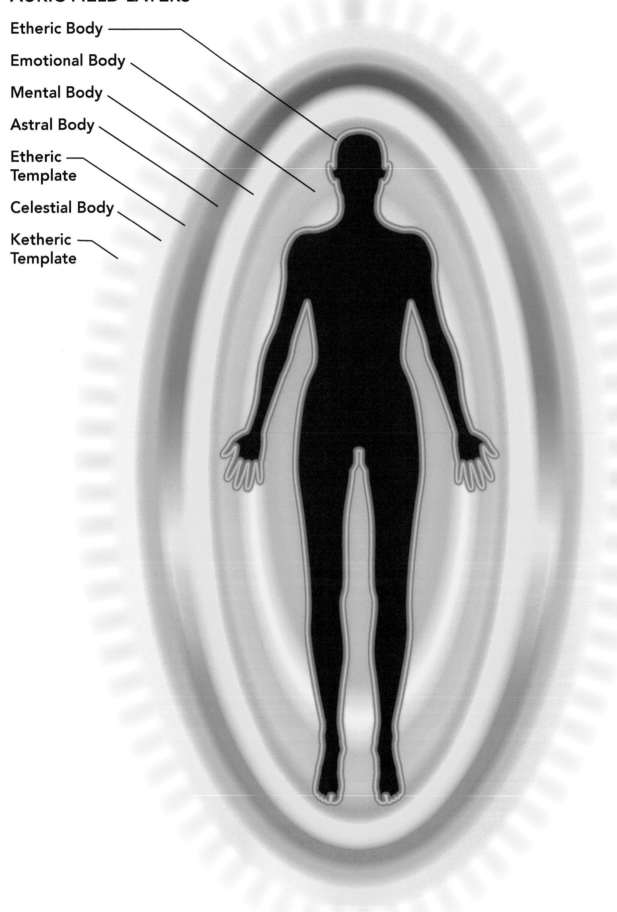

Etheric Body

Emotional Body

Mental Body

Astral Body

Etheric Template

Celestial Body

Ketheric Template

BREATH OF ARJUNA

Arjuna, the son of the god Indra, was the third of five brothers and was renowned for his archery skills; he is considered a heroic archer in Hindu legend. His name means *"bright"* or *"shining."* He is most remembered for the ethical dilemma he faced during a battle involving a branch of his family. It is explained in the sacred Hindu text that Arjuna became aware of the nature of the universe, devotion, and the importance of the right course of action *(dharma)*. All actions must be approached as a form of service to the Divine. Arjuna's acceptance of these principles, even though it involved fighting members of his own family, exemplifies true devotion to the Divine. He symbolizes the qualities of focus and clear vision.

Breath of Arjuna is a simple yoga movement which connects breath, body, mind, spirit, and the imagination.

Another version of this practice consists of three phases:
Shedding what is not needed at the present time.
Drawing in desired qualities, feelings, and power for our personal next step.
Radiating our personal spiritual qualities that we wish to bring to the world.

Movement:

Cross hands with palms touching at the Root Chakra.

Inhale, moving arms up above the Crown Chakra.
I am a Lotus Flower growing upward

Exhale, open arms into a "T."
Soaring through the Sky

Inhale, palms up.
I am open to Surrender

Exhale, carry right arm over to left side.
and to flow

Inhale, moving arms to center.
I move the water

Exhale, move arms to the right side.
and the water moves me

Inhale, left arm open in front continuing to form a "T." *Until I am open*

Exhale, arms down in front.
Until I am free

Repeat the moves to the right side.

BECOMING A MAHA REIKI® MASTER PRACTITIONER/TEACHER

This next level of personal, spiritual, and professional awareness, discipline, training, growth, and development is exciting and carries unlimited potential! Becoming a Maha Reiki® Master Practitioner/ Teacher can support and continue to change your Life and everyone around you, in a positive, compassionate manner. As each of us grows and heals on our personal journey, more doors, possibilities, and joy become available and present. Shadows become less scary when faced, healed, and released with compassion. Obstacles dissolve. New, lighter energy becomes available. Looking with new eyes and understanding guides our every thought and movement. All of these things began to happen the moment you decided to begin your Reiki journey! *Shinpiden*, mystery teaching, is the name for this class and teacher in Japanese. Following the movement of our own personal mysteries as we gain knowledge and insights through compassionate training, is our teaching. As we solve one mystery, another opens. New layers unfold as quickly as the ones before them are solved. The joy of movement and growth is boundless! We will gain the knowledge and compassion to assist and guide others on their journey through their own mysteries of Life.

We will cover the basics of teaching and using all three levels of Maha Reiki®, which includes Usui, Tibetan, and advanced Maha techniques for healing. Manuals for each level are provided. Additional manuals can be ordered as you begin to teach, if you so desire. Many of you may not have plans to teach Reiki, yet inevitably, by sharing with others in conversations, you will be teaching! Living by example, you will be teaching! The opportunities will become endless. The receiving of the four Maha Master symbols can greatly enhance your personal and professional Life, no matter what you currently do or grow into. You have made the decision to enhance your move forward!

There are many Reiki Schools and methods of teaching. The length of training and time spent in classes has experienced a large swing, even since the first teachers began teaching. Maha Reiki® offers a full weekend training for each level. We feel it is important to have a basic history of Reiki, a good strong understanding of energetic healing, develop a deeper personal spiritual connection, learn meditation and chanting to enhance growth in daily practice, and be supported by your Teachers. Continuing education through Reiki Circles is offered and encouraged. Growing and integrating new levels of vibration into one's energetic system is at a personal pace. Too much too soon can create burn-out of the nervous system. This is why daily practice and growth is encouraged and taught, to enhance an optimal foundation of inner strength and understanding.

And now, the new you begins!!!

MEDICINE BUDDHA/TIBETAN REIKI ROOTS

Since 2012, the practice of chanting Medicine Buddha mantra has been an integrated practice in all of my ancient Cranial healing practice from Tibet, Reiki, and other forms of energetic healing work. In my original Usui Reiki training, Tibetan Reiki was briefly mentioned in the modern history of Reiki practice. Over the years, I have found it very beneficial in all of my practices to silently chant the Medicine Buddha mantra. Reiki and Cranial students have also experienced increased vibration, intuitiveness, and effectiveness in their sessions by silently chanting Medicine Buddha mantra.

In 2016, a spiritual journey to Bhutan to meet with His Holiness Ngawang Tenzing Rinpoche changed my life, my personal and professional daily practice, and my teaching. Receiving Medicine Buddha teachings, empowerments, attunements, and being adopted into his lineage and given a most honorable Tibetan name, opened new doorways and possibilities for myself, my practice, and my teachings. Medicine Buddha empowerments are now included in the Maha Reiki® attunements.

During another spiritual journey to Bhutan in 2018, I was honored to meet again with His Holiness Ngawang Tenzing Rinpoche several times, for teachings, empowerments, and guidance in being a teacher. This experience has heightened and strengthened the empowerments I have been given permission to pass on to others.

Upon further investigating the roots of Reiki in Tibet, I uncovered some interesting facts. The Reiki laying of hands for healing is very similar to an ancient method used by Tibetan Buddhists who follow the teachings of healing from the Medicine Buddha practice. The empowerments, giving others the ability to perform this healing method, are passed from teacher to student through the Medicine Buddha teachings. These teachings include intention, chanting, hands-on empowerments, and attunements. There appear to be many Tibetan symbols used in the healing practice of healing with touch.

Mikao Usui was a practicing Buddhist. Perhaps through his intention and his 21-day fast on the sacred Buddhist location of Mount Kurama, Usui tapped into this ancient, powerful, energetic healing realm during his mystical experience, and received the empowerments.

Iris Ishikura, Takata's cousin and student, studied with a Buddhist Monk, worked with energetic healing, and used Tibetan symbols in her practice. Arthur Robertson, her student, teaches and uses the Tibetan symbols. These symbols and methods were also taught by their student, William Lee Rand.

ༀ་སྨན་བླ་བྷེ་ཀན་ཙེ་མ་ཧཱ་བྷེ་ཀན་ཙེ་རཱ་ཛ་ས་མུ་གཏེ་སྭཱ་ཧཱ

MEDICINE BUDDHA MANTRA

TAYATA OM BHEKANDZE BHEKANDZE MAHA BHEKANDZE RANDZA SAMUNGATE SOHA

In Tibetan pronunciation, the mantra is as follows:

Tad-ya-ta Om Be-kan-dze Be-kan-dze Ma-ha Be-kan-dze Ra-dza Sa-mung-ga-te So-ha
"Hail! Appear, O Healer, O Healer, O Great Healer, O King of Healing!"

Tayata - means gone beyond
Om - means jewel holder, auspicious one
Bhekandze Bhekandze - means calling Medicine Buddha twice
Maha Bhekandze - means greatness of Medicine Buddha
Randza Samungate - means perfectly liberated or awakened
Soha - means dissolves in me

The Medicine Buddha Mantra can help us to eliminate problems, unhappiness, and suffering. It helps us to gain success, happiness, and promotes inner growth and development.

It is believed that any living being who hears the name of Medicine Buddha never gets reborn in the lower realms - that is the benefit, the power of just hearing the name, the mantra. The reason there is so much power is due to Medicine Buddha's compassion. In the past when he was a bodhisattva, he made so many prayers and dedications with strong compassion in his name, for wishes to be fulfilled and to bring happiness.

MEDITATION TO PREPARE FOR MASTER ATTUNEMENT

Draw all of your symbols, Cho Ku Rei, Sei Heki, and Hon Sha Ze Sho Nen, into your hands, tapping each symbol three times. Tap the symbols into each chakra three times. Ask for your Highest Light Guides and guardians, from Great Source, to join you in this meditation and the receiving of the Maha Reiki® Master symbols. Ask for your Spirit to open and clear to receiving this attunement.

Sit comfortably, feet flat on floor, spine straight, hands in Gassho, thumbs at heart center, relax your shoulders, close your eyes, and breathe long and deep.

Feel your breath coming up from the Earth Star, through your feet, your ankles, your knees, your hips, up through all of your chakras. As your breath reaches your crown, slowly exhale all tension or tightness you have noticed along the way. Opening your crown, flowing up through your Star Chakra, allow your spirit to connect to the highest, brightest, whitest light as you exhale. Feel yourself diving into the great center of the brightest, whitest light you can imagine. As you exhale, this light is pouring through you, touching every cell inside and outside of your body. This light is bathing and circling around, cleansing and strengthening your auric field and flowing deep into the earth. Repeat this breath five times, until you feel yourself being held in divine light and yet grounded and held by the mother Earth.

Now lightly place your tongue on the roof of your mouth, lightly contract the Hui Yin.

In your mind's eye, see the power symbol Cho Ku Rei in the brightest, shimmering gold light, sitting in your crown chakra. Feel the symbol vibrating, radiating and amplifying the power of divine energy into your crown with shimmering golden light. With the next exhale, allow the Cho Ku Rei symbol to slowly begin moving downward, into your third eye. Feel your third eye vibrating and opening to greater seeing capacity. As you inhale, move the symbol to your throat chakra. Feel the symbol vibrating and opening your throat to receiving greater volumes of golden light. As you exhale, move the symbol to your heart chakra. Feel the heart opening and growing, being replenished and nourished with spinning golden light. Inhale deeply and move the symbol to your power center. Feel the vibration of the symbol radiating golden light, replenishing, opening this chakra. Exhale deeply and move the symbol to your sacral chakra. Feeling this chakra opening, vibrating, and radiating golden light. Inhale deeply, moving the symbol to your root chakra. Feeling the grounding of this energy into your energetic system and your body.

Take several long deep breaths, feeling all of the chakras connected, open, and glowing with this energy.

Now, with a long deep breath, allow the gold, shimmering Cho Ku Rei to begin a journey from your root up the back of the chakras, resting in the sacral chakra. Feel the energizing vibration here. Exhale, moving up to the back of your power center. Continue to feel the spinning, energizing vibration of the symbol. Inhale deeply and move the symbol to the back of the heart chakra, allowing healing filled with golden light in this area. Exhaling, move the symbol to the back of the throat chakra, opening and healing this area. Inhale deeply, moving the symbol to the back of the third eye. Feel the growing sensation of being able to see the past more clearly. Exhale slowly, and move Cho Ku Rei to your crown chakra. Feel the sensation of greater amounts of Divine energy, flowing down from the Cosmos, being amplified with golden shimmery light from the symbol in your crown.

Repeat this rotation three times, at your own breath rate, until you finish. Relax your hands in your lap, palms up. Leave the golden Cho Ku Rei sitting in your crown. Release your tongue and the Hui Yin.

Repeat the entire above process with Sei Heki, for three long breaths. Start with your tongue touching the roof of your mouth and Hui Yin slightly contracted. Relax your hands when completed. Leave the shimmering Cho Ku Rei and Sei Heki resting above your crown.

With your hands resting in your lap, palms up, eyes closed, envision Hon Sha Ze Sho Nen around two feet in front of your body. It is large, the length from your crown to your root chakras. It is glowing in the brightest, gold, shimmering color. Breathe long and deep, feeling the vibration of this symbol pouring through your auric field layers, radiating through every cell of your body. Continue this breathing and meditating on the vibration of this symbol for several minutes. Now, with each inhale, move the symbol a little closer to your body. Slowly, breathe the symbol into your body. It now fuses energetically to your spinal column, nesting and holding all of your chakras.

You are now vibrating from the inside outward. As you continue to breathe slowly, be aware of the other symbols amplifying your Divine connection, flowing through your crown. You are now open, all times, all dimensions are one.

Bring your hands back to your heart, in Gassho. You are now prepared to receive your Maha Reiki® Master attunement! Many Blessings!!!

FUNCTION/GOVERNOR
CHANNELS

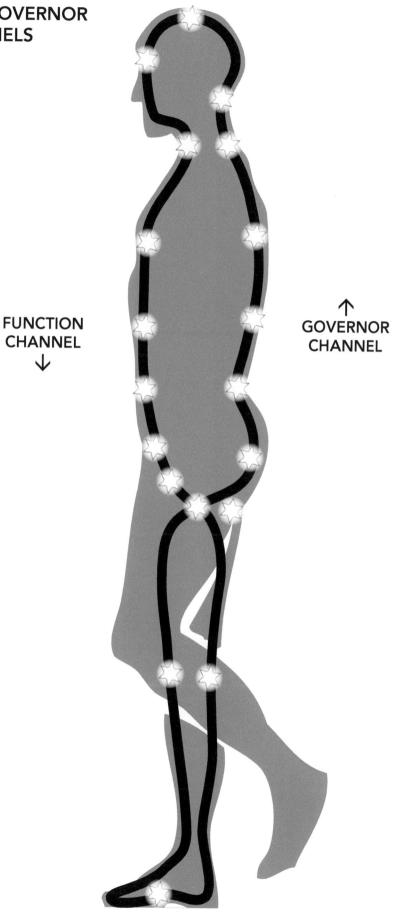

FUNCTION
CHANNEL
↓

GOVERNOR
CHANNEL
↑

Francene Hart

THE MAHA REIKI® MASTER SYMBOLS

The Maha Reiki® symbols include the original three Reiki symbols from Mikao Usui, the master Reiki symbol added by Mrs. Takata, the two Tibetan master symbols added by Iris Ishikura and Arthur Robertson, and the master symbol OM, used in Medicine Buddha empowerments. The use of all seven of these tools in a private session, giving empowerments, or attunements is very powerful. Each symbol represents and carries its own specific, multi-dimensional vibrational energy coming from infinite, Divine Source. As each of us grow in our daily practice, our vibrational frequencies and ability to expand the healing energy of these symbols grows to greater and greater potential. There are no limits to the capabilities, potential of these energetic tools. The ability for each of us to open our minds to infinite, multi-dimensional concepts will change our lives and our practice. The time is now. We are the future. And because the past, present, and future are all happening at once, what appears to be ancient knowledge is really ever-present, waiting to be tapped into!!

The addition of four powerful symbols into your energetic system at once can create many physical symptoms or energetic releases on many levels. Healing can begin to take place where congestion has been held physically, emotionally, mentally, and spiritually. Be aware, gentle, and kind to yourself. Recognize, process, release, and fill with the support from the new symbols and your Reiki Community. You have said yes to this journey. Raising your vibration and energy to higher levels of consciousness can open doors you never knew existed. Grow and integrate at a pace manageable to yourself, your highest good, moment to moment. This practice comes from pure compassion and highest light. Allow yourself to relax, breathe, and receive what is flowing within and around you.

Welcome once again to support, through this practice, to your journey as a seeker and a healer!

Usui Dai Ko Myo   Tibetan Fire Serpent   Tibetan Dai Ko Mio   Master OM Symbol

USUI DAI KO MYO
MASTER SYMBOL

Dai

Ko

Myo

The Master symbol Dai Ko Myo was introduced into the Usui Reiki practice by Mrs. Takata. Usui himself used only the three symbols you learned in Level Two Reiki. This symbol existed long before Mrs. Takata incorporated it into her Reiki teachings. Consisting of three Japanese Kanji characters, it has many similar meanings: "Great, Bright, Light," or "Treasure house of great beaming light," or " Great beaming light, shine on me."

The use of this Master symbol creates a higher connection to an even more refined vibration, higher consciousness, Divine Source. The use of Dai Ko Myo therefore enhances and can greatly amplify the power of the other three Reiki symbols. Using this symbol in a Reiki session can be highly beneficial for both the giver and receiver, taking the work to higher light levels. We recommend using the symbol to begin and end a session. Using the symbol at any time during a session, particularly when addressing congested energy, greatly adds comfort and amplified supportive energy. The symbol has a great grounding effect. Chanting the master symbol can strengthen and amplify any thought or intention. It directly affects your spiritual connection, raising consciousness to "seeing more clearly."

Dai Ko Myo is used when giving attunements and empowerments. The amplification of this great connection to highest light opens doors and blockages that have been waiting to be released. It can be used as a quick but powerful blessing over everything you eat, drink, think, and do! The uses and power of Dai Ko Myo are unlimited. Open your heart and mind and allow the energy to flow for highest good. You are the vehicle.

TIBETAN FIRE SERPENT
MASTER SYMBOL

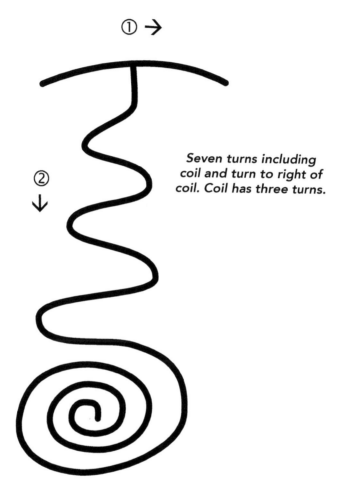

Seven turns including coil and turn to right of coil. Coil has three turns.

Tibetan Fire Serpent is another Tibetan symbol introduced by Arthur Robertson, used in his Raku Kei Reiki. Once again, this symbol feels beyond time, ancient. Because so much information was verbally passed down for eons from Tibetan Masters to students, and writings and monasteries destroyed by the Chinese invasion, we have no idea of the age or origin of this and so many other healing symbols. There is hearsay that over three hundred Tibetan healing symbols were used.

Tibetan Fire Serpent is used in the giving of attunements and empowerments. Draw the arc over the crown of the client or student, and coiling down, around the chakras, seven turns (includes turn to begin the coil) with the coil having three turns over the root chakra. This opens and connects the chakra system, allowing it to open and be ready to receive energy. The symbol is very beneficial in healing sessions for opening pathways to release congested energy. Follow your intuition and allow the symbol to guide as you practice!

TIBETAN DAI KO MIO
MASTER SYMBOL

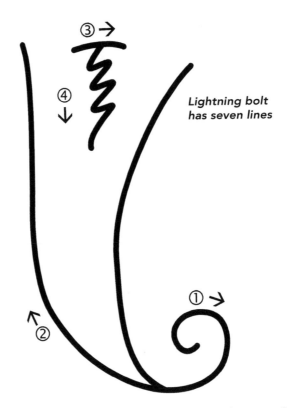

Lightning bolt has seven lines

This Tibetan symbol, Dai Ko Mio, was introduced to Reiki by Arthur Robertson. He not only was a student of Iris Ishikura, but had studied and taught a form of Tibetan shamanism, which had roots in Tibetan Buddhism. This ancient practice of healing with hands was very similar to those that Mikao Usui brought down from Mt. Kurama. He combined the two practices into what is called Raku Kei Reiki. The blending of these symbols and two Reiki practices together has enhanced what we now use in our attunement method, passing empowerments to a student or a client.

The cup is a curling upward movement of two strokes. The energy or lightning bolt has seven lines coming down from Source. Our seven Chakras? Our vessel and the filling of Divine energy?

We feel the Tibetan Dai Ko Mio Master symbol is beyond time, beyond ancient. The vibration feels very feminine, gentle, yet powerful and compassionate. Used in a private session, the symbol can amplify the other symbols to greater healing potential. Drawn from root to crown, opening the pathway for amplified Divine energy to fill the client! It can be easily sent with the eyes or breath. Many techniques that we will learn in this class will be enhanced with this symbol. Once again, the power of this symbol is unlimited, vast. We only need to set the intention, be open and let the amount of healing vibration flow freely!

THE MASTER OM SYMBOL

The Sanskrit word OM is considered by many as the Master of all Master Symbols. OM is used in the Karuna Reiki® and Medicine Buddha empowerments we have received. We have used the OM symbol to enhance the giving of attunements and empowerments for many years now. OM is the word we have student and clients chant when they have no other word to open their throat chakras or to bring themselves into balance. There is a belief of many that OM is the word, the vibration, the sound, that brought Life into creation. With this belief, OM makes everything in creation connected! OM is the sound vibration of spiritual power. In Tibetan practice, OM is three letters: A, U, M. These represent a person's impurity of body, speech, and mind, and at the same time symbolize the exalted body, speech, and mind of the Buddha energy. Chanting AUM, or OM, greatly raises one's vibration, awareness, and spiritual connection.

EXERCISES FOR SYMBOLS

Each symbol carries a different vibration. With the following exercises, we will explore how each symbol feels to send and receive. This sensation may vary, but the subtleness will carry a signature.

Bring your hands to Gassho, thumbs at your heart. Close your eyes. Breathe in long and deep, silently chanting Usui Dai Ko Myo. Draw the symbol into each hand, tapping three times after drawing, repeating the name silently each time. Draw the symbol into each chakra, tapping three times and repeating the name silently.

Bring your hands back to Gassho. Close your eyes and feel the Usui Dai Ko Myo energy between your hands, flowing up to your crown, back down through your heart chakra, and out your hands. Envision the Usui Dai Ko Myo energy filling your auric field. Relax your arms down to your lap. Feel the energy streaming through your crown, pulsating all around your auric field, throughout your body and down to your feet.

Separate into pairs and face your partner. One of you is the receiver and one of you is the sender. The receiver sits comfortably, with hands on thighs, palms up and eyes closed. The sender leans forward, draws Usui Dai Ko Myo slightly above each knee, tapping in three times and silently repeating the name of the symbol. Place your cupped hands lightly on the receiver's knees. Eyes closed, crown chakra open, flow the Dai Ko Myo Reiki energy into your partner's knees. The touch is so light, like a butterfly landing. Do this for a few minutes. Notice any sensation that may be occurring.

The sender disconnects and sits back. Repeat this exercise, trading positions with your partner. Once completed, each student shares the receiving and sending experience with the class.

Sit back and bring your hands to Gassho, thumbs at your heart. Close your eyes. Breathe in long and deep, silently chanting Tibetan Dai Ko Mio. Draw the symbol into each hand, tapping three times after drawing, repeating the name silently each time. Draw the symbol into each chakra, tapping three times and repeating the name silently.

Bring your hands back to Gassho. Close your eyes and feel the Tibetan Dai Ko Mio energy between your hands, flowing up to your crown, back down through your heart chakra, and out your hands. Envision the Tibetan Dai Ko Mio energy filling your auric field. Relax your arms down to your lap. Feel the energy streaming through your crown, pulsating all around your auric field, throughout your body and down to your feet.

Face your partner. One of you is the receiver and one of you is the sender. The receiver sits comfortably, with hands on thighs, palms up and eyes closed. The sender leans forward, draws Tibetan Dai Ko Mio slightly above each knee, tapping in three times and silently repeating the name of the symbol. Place your cupped hands lightly on the receiver's knees. Eyes closed, crown chakra open, flow the Tibetan Dai

Ko Mio Reiki energy into your partner's knees. The touch is so light, like a butterfly landing. Do this for a few minutes. Notice any sensation that may be occurring.

The sender disconnects and sits back. Repeat this exercise, trading positions with your partner. Once completed, each student shares the receiving and sending experience with the class.

Bring your hands to Gassho, thumbs at your heart. Close your eyes. Breathe in long and deep, silently chanting Tibetan Fire Serpent. Draw the symbol into each hand, tapping three times after drawing, repeating the name silently each time. Draw the symbol into each chakra, tapping three times and repeating the name silently.

Bring your hands back to Gassho. Close your eyes and feel the Tibetan Fire Serpent energy between your hands, flowing up to your crown, back down through your heart chakra, and out your hands. Envision the Tibetan Fire Serpent energy filling your auric field. Relax your arms down to your lap. Feel the energy streaming through your crown, pulsating all around your auric field, throughout your body and down to your feet.

Face your partner. One of you is the receiver and one of you is the sender. The receiver sits comfortably, with hands on thighs, palms up and eyes closed. The sender leans forward, draws Tibetan Fire Serpent slightly above each knee, tapping in three times and silently repeating the name of the symbol. Place your cupped hands lightly on the receiver's knees. Eyes closed, crown chakra open, flow the Tibetan Fire Serpent Reiki energy into your partner's knees. The touch is so light, like a butterfly landing. Do this for a few minutes. Notice any sensation that may be occurring.

The sender disconnects and sits back. Repeat this exercise, trading positions with your partner. Once completed, each student shares the receiving and sending experience with the class.

Sit back and bring your hands to Gassho, thumbs at your heart. Close your eyes. Breathe in long and deep, silently chanting Om. Draw the symbol into each hand, tapping three times after drawing, repeating the name silently each time. Draw the symbol into each chakra, tapping three times and repeating the name silently.

Bring your hands back to Gassho. Close your eyes and feel the Om energy between your hands, flowing up to your crown, back down through your heart chakra, and out your hands. Envision the Om energy filling your auric field. Relax your arms down to your lap. Feel the energy streaming through your crown, pulsating all around your auric field, throughout your body and down to your feet.

Face your partner. One of you is the receiver and one of you is the sender. The receiver sits comfortably, with hands on thighs, palms up and eyes closed. The sender leans forward, draws Om slightly above each knee, tapping in three times and silently repeating the name of the symbol. Place your cupped hands lightly on the receiver's knees. Eyes closed, crown chakra open, flow the Om Reiki energy into your partner's knees. The touch is so light, like a butterfly landing. Do this for a few minutes. Notice any sensation that may be occurring.

The sender disconnects and sits back. Repeat this exercise, trading positions with your partner. Once completed, each student shares the receiving and sending experience with the class.

Everyone cuts the energy and returns to their seats. Now we will focus on one student at a time. This student sits comfortably, with their palms facing up on their thighs. The rest of the class places their hands, palms cupped and facing outward, at their heart center. The intention is to now flow Reiki energy to the receiver. Do this flow for a few minutes. Go around the room until everyone has had a turn to receive. Once completed, each student shares the receiving and sending experience with the class.

This is a continual flow of light healing energy that can be with you 24/7. This energy will grow daily, as long as you activate your symbols and your Reiki. It will vibrate through and off of your body, affecting everything and everyone around you in a positive manner!

Everyone stand up and do a few aura strengthening exercises, drink water, get some fresh air and walk around.

Usui Dai Ko Myo

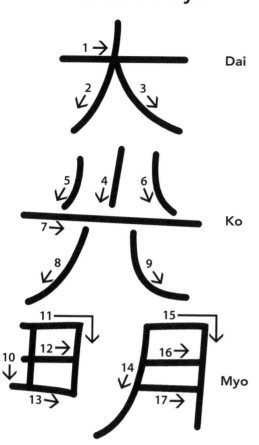

Dai

Ko

Myo

Tibetan Fire Serpent

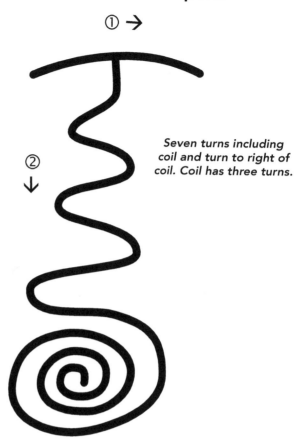

Seven turns including coil and turn to right of coil. Coil has three turns.

Tibetan Dai Ko Mio

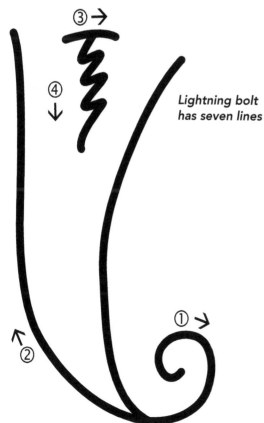

Lightning bolt has seven lines

Master OM Symbol

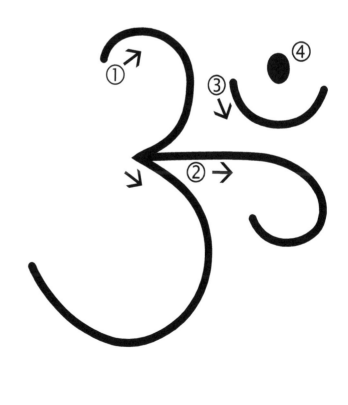

ASSISTING IN THE RELEASE OF ENERGETIC BLOCKAGES AND ATTACHMENTS

Energetic blockages and attachments can take on many forms. The person experiencing this blockage must take a willing and active part in releasing the issue causing their dis-ease or dis-comfort. There may be times when the person is not aware of these blockages or attachments until they come to experience a Reiki session. Other times, they are fully aware of the issues and are seeking assistance in releasing.

As a Reiki Master Practitioner/Teacher, it is important to empower the person with the basic knowledge of their chakra system and auric field. This helps them to understand how energetic blockages develop and are taken into their physical body. Understanding the balance of the physical, emotional, mental, and spiritual bodies is extremely important in the healing process. Genetic inheritance can also play an important role in this process. Depending on the person's belief system, past lives and karma can also come into awareness as being a source of their dis-comfort or dis-ease. Programmed patterns of behavior from our parents, teachers, peers, religious beliefs, employers, and government can create energetic blockages.

Since we do not diagnose illness, it is important to remind the person to continue to work with their current healthcare provider, to monitor their healing process. Once energetic blockages or attachments have been removed, the person's flow of balanced life force energy can create wellness.

There are times when one session is all that is needed. However, as one issue is cleared, another can appear. There can be times when blockages travel through the different chakras, organs of the body, or the layers of the emotional, mental, or spiritual bodies. Each of these areas will need to be addressed.

There can also be moments when the blockage or attachment is persistent in staying. When this happens, this question needs to be asked: Does the blocked energy or attachment have a message for the person, the host, carrying the energy? If this is the case, and the message is not revealed during the session, empower the person to go within themselves on a deeper level, such as with meditation, prayer, connecting to their Highest Divine Source, and ask for the meaning. The unique personal journey of each person is revealed to themselves, when they are open and willing to listen. This truth may be revealed during the session or when the person is alone in their sacred space. As a Reiki Master Practitioner/Teacher, it is important for you to follow up with this person, to answer questions, give support and offer another session to assist in completing the process.

There are several techniques and methods that we use to assist in the removal of energetic blockages and attachments; we will discuss these at length. As a Reiki Master Practitioner/Teacher, as you connect to the purest, highest light source of Divine consciousness, you may be given guidance not mentioned in this manual. Every person, situation, and session is unique and the guidance will be given as requested. Remember, do not minimize the ability of infinite light healing energy to be present and assist as requested with pure intention and compassion!

METHODS OF RELEASING ENERGETIC BLOCKAGES AND ATTACHMENTS

In this chapter, we will discuss the following:

- *Different methods of releasing energetic blockages.*
- *Multi-dimensions and attachments.*
- *Psychic attack and attachments.*

The above techniques can be performed with the sentient being sitting or laying down, in your presence or long distance. Reiki works on all beings in creation. Before working with any sentient being, for any type or length of session, it is always extremely important for the Reiki Master Practitioner/Teacher to have all of your Reiki symbols activated, your chakras balanced, auric field strengthened, be fully grounded to the Earth energy, and connected to Highest Light Source. Ask permission to do the work with the recipient being. This may be done out loud, if they are present, or psychically, if long distance. Set a clear intention for the highest good of the being you are working with to be accomplished. Do not be attached to the outcome. Ask for your and their highest light guides and guardians to be present. Open your heart chakra to greater compassion and your third eye to greater seeing, knowing. See the Reiki energy pouring out of every cell of your body and your hands expanded with bright light. Set the glow of purest white energy in the space you are working or to which you are sending Reiki. Shimmery colors of gold, silver, or violet may accompany this white glow!

Releasing Energetic Blockages

On some level, physically, emotionally, mentally, or spiritually, most people are aware of some sort of congested energy flow somewhere within themselves. They have contacted you, hoping you can open some doors to their healing. By listening to them speak and watching their body language, they will give you the clues to their discomfort. By asking the questions that come into your mind while you are listening to them speak, the root of the issue will begin to reveal itself. Many times, your ability to listen, with no judgment, allows the person to speak honestly, reveal the truth verbally to themselves. Now the real work begins!

Your person can receive the Reiki session either sitting or laying down. If they decide to lay down, ask if they want to go face up or face down. Remember, face up addresses current issues and face down addresses the past. However, if they are unable to lay face down, laying on their side or face up will still achieve the same result. The session is all about the intention of healing for the person's highest good. Place all of the Reiki symbols slightly above their body, as you have them do the long, deep, calming breath, with their eyes closed. Perform an energetic scan through all the layers of their auric field, noticing any variations or sensations at each level.

If the person has not identified a specific area of discomfort, your energetic scan will generally sense the area. Holding your hands over the area of detection, what knowing, thought, or question has popped into your mind? Questions to ask: How long has this DIS-comfort been going on? How old does it feel? Does it have a shape or color? What sound would it make? Are you truly ready to release this pain, energy, DIS-comfort?? When they answer yes, tell them you are going to assist them by energetically reaching into the space of the discomfort and wrapping the glowing Reiki energy around it. Do this as they take a long deep breath in. As they do a forceful exhale, have them imagine they are blowing out the congested energy. At the same time, pull your hands back, with the glowing Reiki energy holding the congestion, and send the energy in an upward movement to greater, healing light. Do this three times.

Allow your person to rest with some calming breaths. Then ask if the discomfort has changed or disappeared. If it has disappeared, you are done. If it has changed, how has it changed? Repeat the procedure three more times. Once again, has it changed or is it gone? Perhaps it has moved to a different location? Continue with the process, allowing resting time between sequences, until there is resolution or the person is ready to say they are done. Remember, it is also possible the energy still has a message or lesson for the person. As releases take place, healing light energy is filling the space where the congestion resided.

There are times during an energetic scan that you feel the need to "brush away" dense energy. Do this with intention, brushing either to the Earth or to the Light. Clearing shadowing energy makes the area of dis-comfort more visible.

Congested energy can feel stringy at times. This can be assisted to leave by a wrapping, circular motion, then gently pulling out and sending to the Earth or to the Light. We don't have to understand or question the signals we receive. The Reiki energy has its own higher consciousness; we are the tool to follow the guidance.

It is very possible that you may receive guidance through any or all of your senses, as you work with a person. Be in the flow of the information. You can gently inform your person of this information, if it is beneficial for their progress in healing. I always ask my guides to be gentle and show me only what is necessary to know in assisting the healing, not the entire movie! When absolutely necessary, the person will also see or experience, on a subtle level, the information.

There are times when the person's highest light guide/guides will appear to perform the necessary healing work. When Spirit is involved, only their highest connection can assist. This is where the Ascended Masters, Archangels, and other higher dimensional beings show themselves. We set the intention and hold the energy for the healing to happen.

Multi-Dimensions and Attachments

Much information has been written on parallel and multi-dimensions. There will be a sample reading list at the end of this manual for those of you who wish to expand your awareness on this subject. The fourth level of our Auric field, our Astral Body, is the bridge to other dimensions. This is the field psychics tap into for readings. Many of us can "feel the presence" of other beings. Our peripheral vision will catch glimpses of other beings in other dimensions. Ghosts are a frequent sighting in some places. Vortexes are doorways into other dimensions. The study of wormholes in space is another vehicle of dimensional travel. The theories and studies have gone on for centuries. It is time to allow our left brain and western upbringing to "Lighten" up to the existence of other dimensions and realms.

Many energies, entities, or spirits occupy these other realms, dimensions. Some have the ability to cross over, appear, into our own. Fragments of spirit can be lost. As we go through our daily lives, we can pick up unwanted fragments of energy from these other places. This can happen when our auric fields are weak. When we have had illness or trauma in any of our physical, emotional, mental, or spiritual bodies, we can become an easy target for lost or wandering spirits. People who work in hospitals and clinics are constantly exposed. We can drag around attached energy without knowing it. Yes, these attachments can affect our daily lives! Some attachments can make you feel depressed, lost, or just out of sorts.

Daily aura strengthening and cutting/clearing ourselves is as important as brushing our teeth and hair. Teach your children, family members, friends, and clients the exercises. When a person, client, comes into your space for a session, clear them and teach them to continue the process.

Sometimes, attachments make themselves known during a client session. There are times when these attachments are ancestral. When this occurs, I have found it very beneficial to call on Archangel Michael to come with his mighty sword to cut the attachments away and take them back, reconnect them to their Source. This allows the healing for the spirit and the client on the table. Attachments can be of benevolent or malevolent in nature. It is important to keep ourselves clean of all energetic attachments and give our own spirit a clear, pure vehicle for our own journey.

Psychic Attack/ Attachments

Psychic attack and psychic attachments happen in many ways. Being a nice person can unknowingly attract psychic attachments. Sometimes we are the only person who has given a smile to someone, listened to someone's story, held the hand of or been in the room during a loved one's moment of passing, or witnessed a fatal accident. All of these instances are just some examples of being in a place where someone's spirit can attach to us unknowingly.

Many times, a strong auric field and cutting energy daily will take care of these attachments. I have had psychologists and medical doctors, who have knowledge of this possibility, send me patients and clients to assist in their clearing of this phenomenon. Personalities, patterns of behavior, interests, work ethics and quality can be noticeably changed when this occurs. Catastrophic illness can result. Once again, tracking the time of change, what trauma were they witness to, what significant has happened in their life, finds the root of the cause.

Prepare yourself, the space, and the client with the procedure mentioned at the beginning this chapter. It is important to set the intention and call in as many highest light guides and Divine spirit assistance as possible. The reconnection of the fragmented spirit to its Source is the overall desired result. This process may take a while, as the fractured spirit may want to stay with its "host" for many reasons. There are cases where the person has been the host for the attachment for lifetimes. The attachment may not be of this realm, dimension, or even galaxy. The attachment may be afraid. Learning to communicate with the attachment may take some time. Not all attachments know light. Not all beings from darkness are "evil." They just existed in a place void of light and need to be returned to their place of comfort. As a Reiki Master Practitioner/Teacher, clients will be drawn to you with issues you will be able to assist with, as you grow in vibration and understanding of what is truly possible in all of creation.

Intentional psychic attacks are another story. There are many hurting people on this planet who wish intentional harm to others. This can be done through intention, ceremony, thought forms, intense anger, and fear. By using all of the techniques mentioned above, you can assist in the release of this energy.

Impress on your client, or yourself, the importance of daily aura strengthening, cutting, and clearing. Then bring your auric field in closer, pour liquid, shimmering silver rays from the cosmos over your auric sphere of light, making it a liquid, reflective, protective shield. The energy will not be able to locate you, but will be returned to sender!

HEALING WITH SINGING BOWLS

We are constantly vibrating. Our blood flowing through our beating heart creates constant micro vibrations. The breath, as it enters and leaves our bodies, creates constant movement and vibrations. Each organ within our body has its own movement, vibration. Yes, we are vibrational beings.

Congested energy, due to trauma, in any of our physical, mental, emotional, or spiritual bodies, can create a different vibration within our physical body. Once we actually feel the dis-comfort in our physical body, the congestion can be very deep and very strong.

This congestion can also be held in our auric field. The fifth level of our auric field is the Etheric Template. It extends one to two feet beyond the physical body. The Etheric Template is related to the throat chakra, our ability to speak, make sound. Sound creates matter. Sound healing is the most effective in this layer of the auric field. This layer also connects us to higher vibrational dimensions.

The Tibetan Bowls can be used to take the vibration of healing deep into tissues, organs, and bones. Their vibration carries through the auric field and our spiritual, emotional, mental, and finally, our physical body, to assist in the vibrational dissolving of energetic blockages. They have been used for this purpose for over 3,000 years. We have found that incorporating Tibetan Bowls into our Reiki sessions, when needed, has been extremely helpful in the client's healing experience. Suren Shrestha, our teacher, has written a wonderful book on this practice. It is listed in the back of the manual and most beneficial to add to your study.

We are including a few pictures to illustrate some general use of Tibetan Bowls in a Reiki session. The bowls can be played in the auric field, around the body, barely above the body, or directly on the body, depending on what is needed by the client. Highest guidance will direct you.

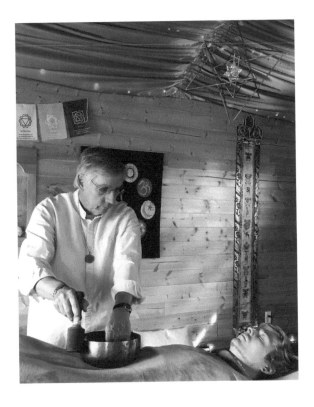

USING CRYSTALS DURING A REIKI SESSION

The Level 1 Maha Reiki® Manual discusses the Chakra system and list crystals used to influence each chakra. The Level 2 Maha Reiki® Manual discusses Reiki healing grids and the potency of using crystals as generators. Reiki is an energetic, vibrational technique that assists in releasing energetic blockages of the body, mind, emotions and spirit. Crystals are a tool than can be used to assist, enhance, and amplify the Reiki healing energy. From ancient times to present, crystals have been recognized and used in a variety of ways. Soaking particular crystals in water can charge the water with healing properties. This water can then be ingested as medicine, working from the inside of the body outward. Crystals worn next to the skin can generate healing and strength. Raising one's vibration during meditation can be assisted with crystals. Crystals can be programed with intention and will continue to hold the programming until cleared, cleansed, and reprogrammed. When holding a crystal during meditation and asking for guidance or information, a crystal can actually pass important knowledge to you. We have found many opportunities during Reiki sessions to effectively use crystals. Most often, the crystal will relay to the practitioner when, where, and how to use it!

How Crystals can be used during a Reiki session:

- Open blockages in areas of congestion, physically, emotionally, mentally, and/or spiritually by being placed directly on the areas of concern.

- Having a client hold a crystal can assist clients who feel they need something material to assist in their process.

- Infusing the crystal with a Reiki symbol and blowing the symbol through the crystal into the area of concern can greatly enhance and amplify the power of the symbol.

- Cradling a Reiki symbol-infused crystal in the palm of your hand, over the area of concern, greatly enhances the energy.

- Placing crystals on the chakras can enhance their flow and balance, open the client's central energetic channel.

- Placing crystals around the client's body can absorb shadowy energy in the auric field.

- Crystals can be used as energetic surgical tools to cut through congested energy.

- Using crystals to close areas that have released large amounts of energy during a Reiki session can add more comfort and ease to the client.

The following pictures demonstrate several ways crystals assist a Reiki session.

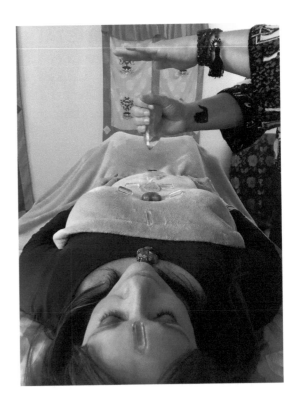

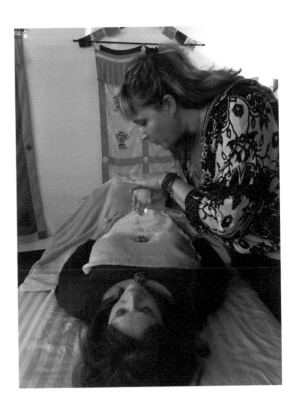

SOUL RETRIEVAL

There is a theory in many belief systems that a Soul, one's personal Spirit, can fracture or splinter during trauma. This trauma can be as old as from being connected to previous lifetimes, coming through the birth canal in current time, and every instance where one has experienced extreme physical, emotional, mental or spiritual trauma, up until this very moment. Not all trauma is remembered, but can be buried deep within one's cellular consciousness. Perhaps one was too young or the trauma was so severe that the mind dissociated from the body. Splintering can sometimes leave one feeling like something is always missing, incomplete, ungrounded, repeating unwanted patterns of behavior, unworthy, many feelings that seem to have no resolution.

Many methods from different indigenous and spiritual healers from around the world are practiced and used to assist the bringing of these fractures back into oneness. The Reiki-guided energy can open channels to enhance this healing process. Over the years of my Reiki practice, I have seen a growing understanding and need for this process to be used during many sessions. Afterwards, the client is reminded to continue the process, as the Spirit can have many, many fractures. Bringing one's Spirit back into wholeness empowers the person to move forward with greater understanding of who they truly are in this lifetime. Forgiveness, releasing, compassion, and feeling safe are important keys to truly embracing self-love and wholeness. Follow up with the client as there are times when a person needs more support, more sessions, to continue to fully recover from some experiences. We also remind them to keep in touch with their medical team of support, as we do not replace them.

Soul Retrieval during a Reiki Session

When talking with your client before their Reiki session, the true reason for the session begins to unfold. Soul retrieval may come up into your intuitive mind. Gently discuss what this means, as many people do not have an awareness of soul/spirit splintering. Once the session begins, continue to be open for the Reiki energy to guide the client and yourself. It is important for the client to make space in their heart, by releasing congested emotions, to receive the reconnecting pieces of Spirit. A client may be able to address one particular instance at a time. Another may be able to go back to the womb and begin. Allowing true guidance to flow through the experience for the client's highest good is the intention of the session.

Calling on the client's Highest Light guides and Guardians, Angels, Ascended Masters, whoever needs to be present in the retrieval, is important before beginning the process. It is not necessary for the client to re-live the trauma. We can ask for the pain to be held by one of their Spirit Guides. Only when the client's Spirit absolutely needs to "see" the trauma to truly heal, will the trauma be shown fully. Many times, the trauma can appear as being seen by a detached witness, a distant showing. With great volumes of Reiki light and compassion flowing, the experience can be healed as it is passing through the consciousness. Comfort can be felt.

Many times I will call on Archangel Metatron , the Keeper of the Akashic Records, to assist in this session. It is said that Metatron wrote each of our own personal Akashic books. Each book contains the history of all of the lives our Spirit has ever lived. Metatron is in charge of the Akashic Library, where all of the books are found. This is the same library that Edgar Cayce would visit during his amazing healing sessions.

The final part of a soul retrieval session is the client's calling back of their Spirit, from whatever trauma has been recognized as causing the fracturing. This can be done by the client repeating in sequences of three: "I love you (client's name), this is where you live, come back to me, clear and clean of attachments, today's date is (day, month, year, and location)." Repeat this several times on the table. When the session is complete, seal, bless, and ask for their highest light guides to continue to support them in this endeavor. Encourage the client to continue to repeat the above words often and daily, as there can be many fractures waiting to be called back to be reunited with their Spirit.

We will now practice this technique. Each client will be unique, so the methods and words will be given specifically for each person. Every session is different. Trust your Highest Guidance for the client's highest good.

PREPARING TO PASS ATTUNEMENTS AND EMPOWERMENTS

Having your Reiki energy activated and the energy of the physical location cleansed and Reiki-charged can greatly enhance the passing of attunements and empowerments to others. The following steps/reminders can empower any intention you are ready to share with others.

- Activate all your Reiki symbols through all your Chakras, including the Earth and Star Chakra
- Draw the symbols on the roof of your mouth
- Open to greater flow of Divine energy, through your Crown and Heart Chakra.
- Be physically, emotionally, mentally, and spiritually prepared.
- Set the energy of the area by infusing all of your Reiki symbols in all seven of the directions
- Call in all of your highest light guides and guardians to assist in the process
- Offer a blessing, prayer of gratitude for this opportunity
- State the intention out loud and chant three long OMs, feeling the vibration fill the area

Empowerments

Empowerments can greatly increase the awareness, focus, and forward movement of the recipient of this gift of Higher vibration. This process is done by infusing the recipient with any or all of the Reiki symbols, depending on the higher guidance you are given in the situation. Empowerments are passed in the same manner as attunements. However, the symbols are NOT placed in the hands, unless the person is Reiki trained. Placing empowerments in the energetic system is very powerful. You must ask permission. Explaining the process is important in preparing the recipient. Passing empowerments can be included in any Reiki session.

Empowerments are given for any and more of the reasons listed below:

- Enhance the recipient's ability to heal to their highest good
- Remove blockages from their physical, mental, emotional, or spiritual bodies
- Focus more clearly
- Set intentions
- Change patterns of behavior
- Raise consciousness levels
- Become more open to possibilities
- Empower goals
- Visualize wellness
- Release fear

The benefits are unlimited, follow the highest guidance for the recipient.

Passing an Empowerment

Energetically prepare yourself and your space.

As mentioned above, empowerments can be given for many reasons. If you want to enhance a Reiki session, we suggest following the outline below, as listed for attunements, without placing the symbols in the hands. You don't necessarily have to infuse a client with all of the symbols, but be guided to which ones are the most important for the intention being set.

There are times when we offer empowerments during special events or occasions. In this instance, we generally give the Medicine Buddha empowerment. The participant can be seated in a chair or sitting on the floor. Follow these steps:

- Have the participant bring their hands to their heart.
- Place one of your hands on one of their shoulders.
- Set your intention of passing Medicine Buddha empowerment to the participant.
- Contract the Hui Yin. Gently place your tongue on the roof of your mouth.
- Placing your hands on their head, leaving a pathway over their crown, blow OM across their crown.
- Place two fingers on their third eye and with the other hand, two fingers on the Mouth of Spirit.
- Visualize tapping OM gently three times into their third eye, silently saying OM. At the same time, visualize the energy being sealed by holding the base of the skull, the Mouth of Spirit.
- With your hands still in these positions, silently chant the Medicine Buddha Mantra.
- Place your hands on the participant's shoulders, feeling the energy flow from your hands into their body.
- Touch and gently squeeze their hands to let them know you are finished.

Attunements

Prepare the space and yourself, as described above.

Have the student sitting in a chair, their feet touching the floor, spine straight. You must be able to walk around the student, as you will be touching them in back, front, and side. Explain to them the process. They will feel you touching their shoulders, tapping, and blowing. Their hands will be in Gassho. When they feel you tap one shoulder three times, they are to lift their hands and place them on their crown.

Now, prepare the student energetically by taking them into a balancing, attunement meditation. Ask them during the meditation to be open to receiving this gift of these Reiki symbols into their energetic system. Each level of the Maha Reiki® manuals has a preparation to receive an attunement meditation you can follow, or use one of your own. As you give more attunements, you will follow your own guidance and flow.

Giving Attunements

You are ready to give and the student/client is prepared and ready to receive.

- Stand behind the student. Place both of your hands on their shoulders. Say a silent intention for the level of Reiki you are about to pass to the student. Call in their highest light guides and guardians to be their witness.

- Holding the energy in their auric field, draw Tibetan Fire Serpent, curving over their crown and curving down and coiling at the Root Chakra. Energetically tap in the symbol three times, silently repeating the name.
- Place your tongue gently on the roof of your mouth and contract the Hui Yin. This position will be held throughout the entire attunement process.
- Open your crown and visualize greater volumes of Divine light flowing through you. This may appear as bright white, shimmering colors, or violet light.
- Energetically draw Tibetan Dai Ko Mio on the back of the student's skull, with the intention that it is further opening their ability to receive a greater vibration of Divine light energy.
- Place your hands directly over the student's crown, leaving an opening between your thumbs and forefingers.
- Look through the opening in your hands, down into the student's Chakra system.
- With a deep, long breath, blow the Tibetan Dai Ko Mio symbol all the way down to their Root Chakra.
- Placing one hand on the student's shoulder, draw the Tibetan Dai Ko Mio symbol above their crown and tap into their energetic system by touching their crown, the back of the third eye and the base of the skull (the Mouth of Spirit). Silently repeat the name of the symbol with each touch.
- Repeat this process with Usui Dai Ko Myo.
- Tap on the student's shoulder three times, the signal for them to raise their hands, in Gassho, to their crown.
- Draw Cho Ku Rei over the tips of the fingers. Tap the symbol into the tips once, move and tap the symbol into the back of the third eye and the base of the skull, silently repeating the symbol's name.
- Do this same movement with Sei Heki, Hon Sha Ze Sho Nen and Usui Dai Ko Myo.
- Move to the front of the student.
- Bring their hands down to the front of their heart and open them. Hold both in one of your hands.

For Level 1 Reiki Students:

- Draw Cho Ku Rei energetically over each of their open hands, tapping into each one three times and silently repeating the name of the symbol.

For Level 2 Reiki Students:

- Draw and tap in, one at a time: Cho Ku Rei, Sei Heki and Hon Sha Ze Sho Nen into their open hands, three times for each symbol.

For Master Practitioner/Teacher Level Reiki Students:

- When the hands in Gassho come to the crown, draw and tap into the finger tips, one at a time: Cho Ku Rei, Sei Heki, Hon Sha Ze Sho Nen, Usui Dai Ko Myo, Tibetan Dai Ko Mio,

Fire Serpent, and OM, following the crown, third eye, and base of the skull. Silently repeat the name of the symbol with each tap.

- Move to the front of the student.
- Bring their hands down to the front of their heart and open them. Hold both in one of your hands.
- Draw and tap three times into the open hands, one at a time: Cho Ku Rei, Sei Heki, Hon Sha Ze Sho Nen, Usui Dai Ko Myo, Tibetan Dai Ko Mio, Fire Serpent, and OM. Silently repeat the name of the symbol with each tap.

For all Levels, once the symbols are placed in the hands:

- Close the student's hands loosely. Take a deep breath. Imagine you are bringing down the greatest volume of Divine light and blow from their crown down to their hands and end at their Heart Chakra.
- Close the student's hands tightly, with one of your hands, at the Heart Chakra level.
- Move to the side of the student, still holding their hands.
- Place your other hand on the back of their Heart Chakra.
- Silently say a welcoming affirmation and blessing. Energetically feel it flowing into their Heart Chakra.
- Move your front hand up to the front of their third eye. Move your back hand to the base of their skull. Visualize sealing the Mouth of Spirit with OM.
- With your hands still in this position, silently chant Medicine Buddha three times.
- Gently hug your student.

Francene Hart

GIVING ATTUNEMENTS 1/4

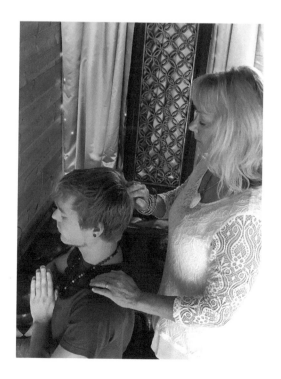

GIVING ATTUNEMENTS 3/4

GIVING ATTUNEMENTS 4/4

CLOSING CEREMONY

This meditation, or one in your own words, can be used at the end of each class or Reiki Circle. Honoring, blessing, gratitude, joining the energy of all others around our Earth and Cosmos, allows everyone to depart supported and connected!

Meditation

Let us all join hands in a circle, right hand up to receive energy and left hand down to send energy. Inhale a very long, slow, deep breath, feeling the energy coming up from deep through the Earth, all the way up through your body. Feel the vastness of your heart chakra. As your breath reaches your crown, slowly exhale while allowing immense amounts of Cosmic Light Energy to flow down through your body and through your hands. As this energy flows from hand to hand to hand, feel the energy building. As this energy builds, it begins to flow out of every cell of your body. The energy flows deep into the Earth. The energy flows and meets the waters of the Earth, the streams, rivers, oceans, flowing at light speed, carrying the healing energy to the water and all of her creatures. As the water continues the flow, the mist, fog, and rain rise, carrying the healing energy to the land. Moisture forming over the land, moving, carrying healing energy, flowing at the speed of light, touching everything. All sentient beings, stones, soil, plants, everything is receiving the healing energy. The energy is flowing up through the air, into the ethers, healing the air we breathe. The vibration of the energy and light is connecting with all the other beings around our Earth, doing similar practice. As we raise the vibration through connection, we begin to poke holes through the fabric of suppression and control that has surrounded our Mother Earth for thousands of years! We are bridging, bringing in higher consciousness to assist the Human species in its quantum leap of consciousness, to benefit the survival all species. May our Earth once again flow with love and compassion for All. As we hold and grow this energy, may it radiate into the cosmos and join with all other beings doing similar practice, in all of creation.

Such gratitude and honor for each and every one of us who have physically attended this weekend. Such gratitude and honor for all of our Highest Light Spirit Guides, Guardians, Angels, Ascended Masters, and Ancestors who love us unconditionally, who have been present to assist and support us. Such gratitude for this opportunity to receive, give, share, and honor this Divine energy with one another. So much gratitude for this Community of like minded people.

Guide each one of us safely to our homes. May we rest and integrate all we have received. And may we always remember, we are not alone.

Namaste   Sat Nam

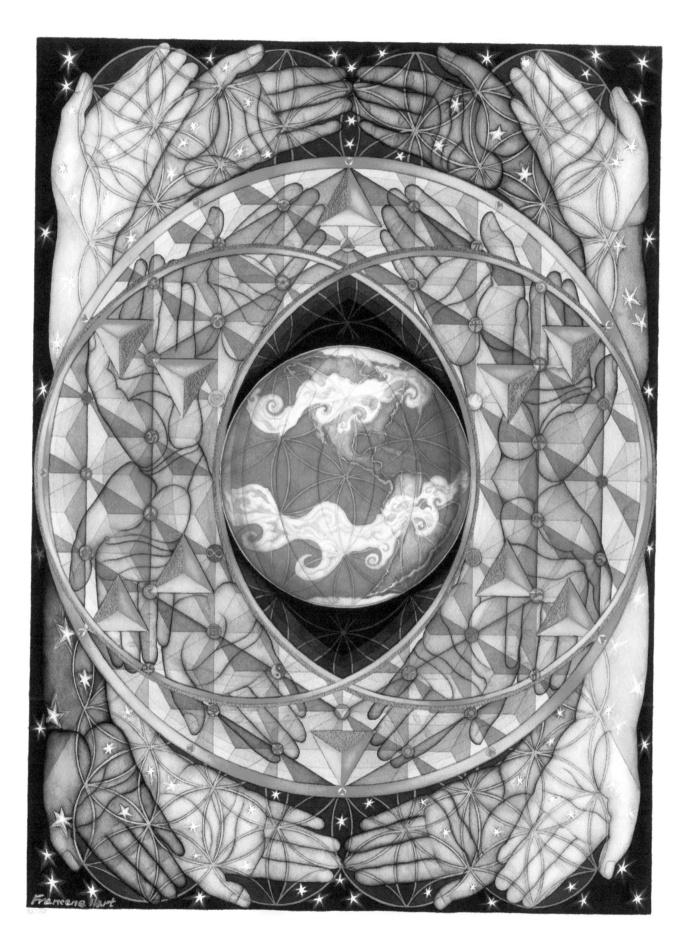

Francene Hart

CLASS OUTLINE MAHA REIKI® LEVEL 1

- Welcome and Introductions
- Students tell a little about themselves and why they are taking the class
- Go outside and do either smudging or aura strengthening to prepare for class
- Test the strength of each Student's Auric field, before and after the exercise
- Remind the Students to stay well hydrated all day
- Provide light snacks to keep Students nourished and energy up
- Discuss Code of Ethics
- Discuss how you (teacher) discovered Reiki and Donna's story if relevant
- Discuss Reiki Kanji Symbols
- Discuss Reiki History
- Discuss Master Lineage Chart – it is now their lineage
- Discuss Flower of Life/Sacred Geometry
- Discuss The Five Precepts – have class repeat precepts for several minutes, together. Discuss the importance of repeating these, or ones they choose daily.
- Read the energy of the Students and take breaks as energy slumps
- Discuss Chakras
- Illustration – Wheels of Light by Francene Hart. Have the students really take the time to look, feel, interpret what they see and feel as they gaze at this picture...perhaps write their thoughts on page 14.
- Review each Chakra: Name, Color, Mantra, etc.
- Illustration – Spinning Chakras - explain how the chakras spin clockwise on the front (current issues), counter-clockwise on the back (issues from the past), and meet in the center, the central channel. When all the chakras are spinning in balance front and back, as they meet in the central channel, the energy, or Kundalini, can flow!
- Lead class in Chakra Balancing Meditation
- Illustration – Auric Field. General discussion of text, just to familiarize with the layers.
- Lead class in Aura Strengthening Exercise
- Take a break, prepare for lunch. Everyone shares meal together.
- Students take a short time out break after cleaning up from lunch.
- Discuss Reiki: What It Is and How It Works
- Explain Illustration: Receiving Attunement by Francene Hart

- Discuss Reiki Attunement
- Lead class in Meditation for Attunement
- Perform Attunements
- Allow Students to integrate the attunement, everyone staying in meditative energy. Give them time to journal. Once everyone has come back to focus, have sharing time for those who wish to share their experience during the attunement.
- Lead class in Self Reiki - This will end the first day of class.

SECOND DAY Level 1 Class
- Welcome and Check in with Students
- How did they sleep? Dreams? Did they self Reiki this morning? How do they feel now?
- Do Aura Strengthening
- Make sure everyone has something to drink
- Do Chakra Balancing Meditation. While Students are feeling the flow, let them sit quietly for a few minutes.
- Go into Reiki activation meditation
- Have students stand up and Reiki the room
- Take a break
- Review the process of detecting the flow of energy, scanning. Practice by pairing up, one seated in chair. The standing student practices feeling the flow of energy, scanning front and back of their partner. Allow their hands to settle where they are called to settle. Switch partners.
- Seated Reiki: Practice hand positions
- Discuss cutting the energy from your hands and body after giving Reiki
- Lunch
- Discuss setting the energy of the space before giving a Reiki Session
- Review Anatomy for Reiki
- Reiki Clinic Session
- Set up the tables. Divide into groups of two or three. Explain how to bolster.
- Practice detecting the flow of energy through each auric field layer
- Hand Positions for others. Have students hold each position for minimum of one minute. Explain they are learning the ABCs of Reiki hand positions. They will be writing chapters by the end of class today! Each student receives a session on front and back.
- Discuss Animal Reiki
- Discuss Client Information Form
- Discuss Daily Practice
- Discuss Sacred Space
- Discuss Reiki Circle
- Closing
- Student questions and comments
- Closing Circle

CLASS OUTLINE MAHA REIKI® LEVEL 2

- Welcome and Introductions
- Students tell a little about themselves and why they are taking the class
- Go outside and do either smudging or aura strengthening to prepare for class
- Test the strength of each Student's Auric field, before and after the exercise
- Remind the Students to stay well hydrated all day
- Review Code of Ethics
- Review Master Lineage
- Chant the Five Precepts for several minutes
- Chakras, short discussion
- Review Illustrations
- Discuss Auric Field
- Take a break
- Have everyone move their chairs into a circle
- Lead class in Chakra Balancing Meditation, have them sit in the energy for a few minutes
- While still in meditation, take them into Reiki activation meditation
- Lead class in meditation for Level 2 attunements
- Perform Level 2 attunement
- Allow Students to sit in the energy, continue to meditate, journal, etc.
- Once everyone is back to being present, ask if anyone would like to share
- Discuss Reiki Level 2 Symbols. Share stories for each symbol, use mine, or add your own.
- No drawing symbols until tomorrow
- Closing Circle

SECOND DAY Level 2 Class

- Welcome and Check in with Students
- How did they sleep? Dreams? Did they self Reiki this morning? How do they feel now?
- Do Aura strengthening
- Make sure everyone has something to drink
- Do Chakra Balancing Meditation. While Students are feeling the flow, let them sit quietly for a few minutes.

- Lead them into Reiki activation meditation
- Continue discussion on the symbols and practicing drawing each one
- Take a break
- Pair up Students, so they face each other sitting
- Lead class in Exercises for Symbols. Have each Student talk about each symbol. Can they feel a vibration, sensation?
- Lunch
- Discuss Sending Reiki with Breath. Practice this technique in pairs.
- Discuss Sending Reiki with Eyes. Practice sending Reiki with eyes to each Student, where they sit around the room.
- Discuss Sending Reiki Long Distance
- Reiki Clinic Session. Practice with new symbols and new techniques.
- Closing Circle. (Remind Students to bring a stuffed animal or picture for practice Sunday)

THIRD DAY Level 2 Class

- Welcome and Check in with Students
- How did they sleep? Dreams? Did they self Reiki this morning? How do they feel now?
- Do Aura strengthening
- Make sure everyone has something to drink
- Do Chakra Balancing Meditation. While Students are feeling the flow, let them sit quietly for a few minutes.
- Lead them into Reiki activation meditation, including the new symbols
- Discuss Weaving technique
- Practice weaving
- Discuss Planting Stars and Running Light
- Practice planting stars and running light
- Review Anatomy pages as necessary
- Discuss Louise Hay and Masaru Emoto. Show pictures from Emoto's book.
- Discuss Mantras
- Practice chanting Om Mani Padme Hum for several minutes
- Practice chanting Medicine Buddha for several minutes
- Lunch
- Discuss Crystals
- Discuss Healing Grids. Set up grids.
- Reiki Clinic Session. Practice all new techniques. Everyone receives full sessions.
- Review Daily Practice, Sacred Space, Reiki Circle, and Client Information Form
- Questions and Comments
- Closing Circle

CLASS OUTLINE MAHA REIKI® MASTER TEACHER

- Welcome and Introductions
- Students tell a little bit about themselves (keep to 3 min.) and why they are taking the class
- Go outside and do either or both smudging and aura strengthening to prepare for class
- Remind Students to stay well hydrated all day
- Review Code of Ethics, Lineage, and Precepts
- Discuss and make Pujas
- Take a break
- Chakra Balancing Meditation
- Breath of Arjuna
- Becoming a Reiki Master
- Medicine Buddha discussion and chanting
- Take a break
- Attunement Meditation
- Perform attunements
- Allow each person time to integrate, journal, then share experience
- Take a break, prepare for lunch. Everyone shares meal together.
- Master Symbols and Exercises for each, compare/notice different vibrations
- Question and answer time
- Closing Circle

SECOND DAY Master Class

- Welcome and check in
- Go outside and smudge and/or aura strengthening
- Remind everyone to stay hydrated during the day
- Meditation to activate Master Symbols
- Discuss energetic blockages
- Take a break
- Practice release techniques for energetic blockages
- Review using singing bowls in a Reiki session
- Review using crystals in a Reiki session

- Take a break, prepare for lunch. Everyone shares meal together.
- Practice using crystals and singing bowls in a session
- Take a break
- Soul Retrieval discussion and practice
- Question and answer time
- Closing Circle

THIRD DAY Master Class

- Welcome and check in
- Go outside and do Aura strengthening
- Remind everyone to stay hydrated during class
- Meditation to activate the Master Symbols
- Discuss the passing of Empowerments
- Practice passing empowerments
- Take a break
- Discuss the passing of Attunements
- Practice each level of Reiki attunements
- Question and answer time
- Take a break, prepare for lunch. Everyone shares meal together.
- Review Class Outlines and each level of Maha Reiki® Manuals
- Question and answer time
- Review Daily Practice, Sacred Space, Reiki Circle, Client Information Form
- Question and answer time
- Closing meditation and Circle

PUJA
A PROSPERITY PRACTICE

Puja addresses prosperity on many levels from relationships to finances, feng shui, removing negative energy, and manifesting aspirations. Puja is also a prayer for the welfare of others or for the favorable results of an undertaking in business or personal life. You may also honor loved ones who have passed on, asking the Divine to bring their souls to peace and rest.

How to do it? First purify yourself with a shower or bath. Dress yourself in clean clothes, being careful to avoid the use of any leather objects such as belts, shoes, or wallets. This is a tradition based on avoiding the suffering of sentient beings. Optimally, you should be barefoot, though you may choose to wear socks.

Many items and elements can be included in your personal Puja, which is in your sacred space:
- Water is the most important
- Small container for the water
- Altar table with pictures, statues of ancestors, Guru, deities, guides, etc.
- Bell, gong, or singing bowls
- Incense, holder and lighter
- Vase with flowers
- Small spoon
- Fruit offerings

Once cleansed and dressed, you now take the water container and fill it with water. While filling the container, hold a very sacred intention for the water's use, as blessed water will be used for cleansing and sanctification. Bring it to your sacred altar and spoon a few drops onto the statues or at the base of the picture frames, with the intention of giving the gifts of fresh water to honor your teachers.

Next, light the incense and offer the smoke of the incense to your teachers as you move your hand in a clockwise motion. With the other hand ring the bell, gong, or singing bowl. The sound removes negative energy in your house and it brings consciousness to the present moment. During this time, chant your mantra or focus your intention to manifest your soul's wish. Now place the incense in the holder.

The impact of this water ceremony is very important and you may wish to use the flower dipped in the holy water to sprinkle around the room to cleanse the space if negative energy is present.

Because the holy water is sacred, it will sit on your altar for the remainder of the day. You may pour the water on a plant before getting fresh water the next day.

Only one person needs to perform the Puja for the entire household to benefit from the practice.

DAILY PRACTICE

Take five, 10, 15, 20 or more minutes, whatever you can give, to start your day calm and balanced. Remember, it takes 40 days to establish a new pattern of behavior!

Activate all of your Reiki Symbols

Tap your symbols into your chakras and/or areas of discomfort, upon waking.
I believe showing gratitude and saying the name of the Reiki symbols adds strength to their energy.

Balance your Chakras with the Chakra meditation.

Envision your symbols running through your entire chakra system, assisting in balancing and preparing your energy for the day.

Aura Strengthening

Start every morning with an aura strengthening exercise, as soon as your feet hit the floor!
Place a tightly woven, ever-moving fabric of millions of Cho Ku Rei symbols over your auric field.
For extra protection, pour a liquid silver ray from the Cosmos over your entire auric field, making it as reflective as a mirror! And don't forget to cut, cut, cut away unwanted energy.

Recite your affirmations

Usui Sensei gave us the example of the five precepts. You can use these or create your own. Use your voice! Feel the vibration of the words flowing through your chakras. Feel their vibration through every cell of your body.

Breath

Breath is sacred. It is our life force that flows through every cell of our body. In many cases, traumatic life experiences and stress, no matter what creates it, has taken our breath away. Taking the time to re-train our breath to be full and rich, takes daily practice. Sometimes, moment to moment practice is needed. For ourselves, doing the chakra meditation every morning, and/or during the day, can help keep us balanced, relieve stress and relieve minor physical discomfort.

To self-empower family, friends and others, teach them!
Take the time to take a very long deep breath, up from the bottoms of the feet, all the way up through the body, reaching the top of the head. Exhale out any stress or tightness, nice and slow. Repeat this five times. If the tightness or stress is extreme, blow it out forcefully, with the intention of releasing the stress NOW! This breath can calm and balance immediately. Repeat this breath many times a day, as needed. Relieving stress and minor physical discomfort by breathing is free, has no side effects, and can never be done too much!

Teach this breath technique to everyone you share Reiki with. Start every Reiki session you give with this breath. As they leave a session, remind them to practice the calming breath daily.

Blessing your food and water with Reiki

What we put into our bodies has a direct effect on our bodies: physical, emotional, mental, or Spiritual. Most of the time, we are in control of what we expose ourselves to, as far as food, medicine, liquids, and water are concerned. The choice and purity of those items are personal. Granted, the quality of our choices directly affects our systems. What we can be aware of is this: Reiki energy can purify, cleanse, and bless whatever it is we are about to ingest. Don't forget your pet's food and water too!

Reiki your home and office

Fill your home and office with the intentions of love, light, and protection. Daily infusions of the Reiki energy build, like charging a battery. Each infusion strengthens and amplifies the Reiki energy. Everything will benefit from the higher vibration. Your pets, houseplants, anyone in your space, and the space itself feels the comfort and love.

Those who do not resonate or who wish harm, soon cannot enter your space, or if they do, they don't stay long!

Daily place a dome of Reiki light, infused with your Reiki symbols, over your property, house, and car. Soon, you will realize that every breath and every step you take, is infused with and radiates the positive love, light, and energy of Reiki!

SACRED SPACE

Activate Your Reiki Symbols
Chant Sacred Mantra
Meditate
Set intention for the Day
Open to greater Compassion

Setting aside a sacred space for yourself at home is extremely important. This can be a room, a small section of a room, a chair in the corner of a room that only you use, your private space. Use this space as you begin your daily practice. In the space perhaps you can have an altar, for your sacred pieces, that no one else touches. This can be a small table, a chest, a drawer, something that houses, protects, and honors your personal items. As you begin and end your day, use your sacred space. This space allows you to tune in to your highest good body, mind, emotions, and spirit. Light a small candle each morning, to represent an honor your light for the day. (Be sure to blow out, or put where no harm can be done if left. Small tea lights are perfect for this, as they only last 2 hours)

Sacred space can also be a private, secluded place in nature where you can connect to your highest good. You can go to this place in your mind when the weather or time does not allow you to physically be there.

As part of your daily practice, honoring the seven directions and elements is important. This practice is ancient, has been and is practiced by many worldwide. Setting a circle of intention and protection daily grounds and connects your spirit and your journey. The significance of the directions may vary with different cultures. Research and read other interpretations to find the one that resonates with you.

The following is one belief system: Calling in the grandmothers and grandfathers and guardians of highest good in each of the following directions, create a sacred circle of honor and protection. The North represents the mother Earth and abundance. The East represents the air and the ability to see from higher perspective. The South represents fire and transformation. The West represents water, sustainer and giver of life on this planet. Each of these directions can have an animal totem representing the energy and also a color. Now, the direction of above representing highest consciousness, Great Spirit. The direction of below, as above, so below, highest consciousness. The final direction is found within Self. We are each the final direction. Now, you are ready to greet the day!

REIKI CIRCLE

As a new Reiki Master Practitioner/Teacher, daily practice and symbol activation is important to continue to raise and strengthen your Reiki energy. As you begin to give private Reiki sessions and teach Reiki classes, you will notice the need to create a supportive Reiki Community.

Joining or building a Reiki Community in your area is energetically rewarding and strengthening. Finding like-minded people with similar practices is comforting. We all learn from each other. New students will find comfort and value by attending a monthly (or more often) Reiki Circle. Oftentimes, a Reiki Circle is the only time a new student may work with someone outside of their immediate family. Each person and each session presents new ways the Reiki energy heals. Remember: we are clear and open channels for the Reiki energy to flow to the recipient for their highest good of body, emotions, mind, and spirit. We are not attached to the outcome of their healing, as we do not know their highest good.

Reiki circles can be formed several different ways. Finding an appropriate location is important.

If you have multiple Practitioners, we have found it best to work one on one, or no more than two Practitioners performing the Reiki on the recipient. This means having several tables, if multiple Practitioners are present. If there are others without tables, chair Reiki can be done. Others can hold the group in Reiki energy domes of light.

Some Reiki Circles are open to the public. They can be done in your home (if you are comfortable) or at an office, or public meeting room that allows gatherings. These Circles can be offered for free or for a minimal fee or donation.

We offer regular, monthly Reiki Circles as ongoing education. All Reiki students, all levels, are invited to attend. Everyone has the opportunity to receive, give, and share. Questions are answered. New information is offered. This can be the only opportunity some Practitioners have to work with others.

Many layers of healing can be experienced and discussed. Everyone benefits and grows in their personal practice and understanding of Reiki. A monthly "tune up" is experienced. Everyone benefits!

PRACTICE, PRACTICE, PRACTICE!!!

Never minimize the healing energy of Reiki.

Daily embrace greater volumes of infinite, Divine, unconditional love.

HELPFUL TIPS FOR A SUCCESSFUL REIKI PRACTICE

The Session

- Create a comfortable, safe environment for your session space. Have your healing tools, if you use any, already in your space (music, crystals, bowls, etc.)

- Have client sign a release form.

- Ask the client: Why are you here today? They will divulge important information: Listen to client's words, watch their body language. The proper questions will come to you. Explain a Reiki session, including information on chakras and auric field. Be aware of your time. In some sessions you do more listening, that's what the client may need.

- Lead client to the Reiki table. Get them comfortable with bolsters and covers.

- Upon completion of the session, give the client a few private minutes alone, as you go to bring them a drink. Gently assist the client to sit up. Move them to the end of your table. Keep a hand on their shoulder to keep them steady! If the client is dizzy, kneel and hold their feet until they are grounded. Give them their drink.

- Answer questions client may have from the session. Or, if you have been given a message to relay to them, do this gently. Empower the client with homework, perhaps a breath technique, mantra, or a stretch, so their healing process can continue. HELP them embrace their own power to heal!

- Assist client off of the Reiki table. Ask them if they would like to schedule their next appointment. Remind them to stay hydrated.

- Give them two business cards as they leave – one for their wallet and one to give to a friend.

- Follow up and check in with the client 24-48 hours after their session to see how they are doing, answer any questions.

Soft Marketing

- Always carry your business cards with you! As you have conversations with others, even strangers, the opportunity to talk about the possible healing benefits of Reiki could very well arise. Cards are important!

- Always have your calendar, scheduler with you.

- Facebook, Instagram, posting flyers in coffee shops and yoga studios, are all helpful.

- Offer an introductory discounted session fee.

- Keep a contact list from all clients. Send them a monthly text or email to check in.

- Think about specific groups you may want to introduce yourself to.

- Plan offerings or events around special dates.

- Don't minimize the possibilities or opportunities that surround you, be creative!

CLIENT INFORMATION FORM

I understand that Reiki is a simple, gentle, hands-on energy technique that is used for stress reduction and relaxation. I understand that Reiki practitioners do not diagnose conditions nor do they prescribe or perform medical treatment, prescribe substances, nor interfere with the treatment of a licensed medical professional. It is recommended that I see a licensed physician or licensed health care professional for any physical or psychological ailment I may have.

I understand and believe that the body has the ability to heal itself, and to do so complete relaxation is often beneficial. I also understand that multiple treatments may be necessary to bring my system back into balance.

Privacy Notice:

No information about any client will be discussed or shared with any third party without the written consent of the client or parent/guardian if the client is under the age of 18.

Name: (Please Print)_____ DOB_____

Home Phone: _____ Cell Phone:_____

Address: _____

City, State, Zip:_____

Email:_____

Emergency Contact:_____Phone:_____

Are you currently under the care of a physician? ❑ Yes ❑ No
Have you ever had a Reiki session before? ❑ Yes ❑ No
Are you sensitive to perfumes or fragrances? ❑ Yes ❑ No
Are you sensitive to touch? ❑ Yes ❑ No
Are you on prescription medication? ❑ Yes ❑ No

Do you have any areas of concern?_____

_____

Signed:_____ Date:_____

Parent/Guardian consent if client is under 18 _____

SUGGESTED READING LIST

Andrews, Shirley. *Lemuria and Atlantis.* Woodbury, MN: Llewellyn Publications. 2009.

Becker, Robert O. and Gary Selden. *The Body Electric.* New York, NY: William Morrow. 1985.

Braden, Gregg. *The God Code.* Carlsbad, CA: Hay House, Inc. 2004.

Chopra, Deepak. *The Seven Spiritual Laws of Success.* San Rafael, CA: Amber Allen Publishing. 1994.

Clow, Barbara Hand. *Alchemy of Nine Dimensions.* Charlottesville, VA: Hampton Roads Publishing Company, 2004.

Clow, Barbara Hand. *The Pleiadian Agenda.* Rochester, VT: Bear & Company, 1995.

Hall, Judy. *Crystal Bible 2.* Cincinnati, OH: Octopus Publishing Group, 2009.

Henkle, Duane. *The Ascension Guidebook.* Vancouver, WA: Crystal Triangle Publishing, 2006.

Kenyon, Tom. *The Hathor Material Revised and Expanded Edition.* Orcas, WA: ORB Communications, 1996.

Marciniak, Barbara. *Earth.* Santa Fe, NM: Bear & Company, 1995.

Melchizedek, Drunvalo. *Living in the Heart.* Flagstaff, AZ: Light Technology Publishing, 2003.

Miller, David K. *Arcturians: How to Heal, Ascend and Help Planet Earth.* Flagstaff, AZ: Light Technology Publishing, 2013.

Miller, David K. *Connecting with the Arcturians.* Flagstaff, AZ: Light Technology Publishing, 1998.

Milanovich, Norma J. *We, The Arcturians.* Albuquerque, NM: Athena Publishing, 1990.

Shrestha, Suren. *How to Heal with Singing Bowls.* Boulder, CO: Sentient Publications, 2013.

Todeschi, Kevin J. *Edgar Cayce on the Akashic Records.* Virginia Beach, VA: A.R.E. Press, 1998.

Usui, Mikao and Frank Arjava Petter. *The Original Reiki Handbook of Dr. Mikao Usui.* Twin Lakes, WI: 2011

Villoldo, Alberto. *Soul Retrieval.* Carlsbad, CA: Hay House, Inc. 2005.

Villoldo, Alberto. *Shaman, Healer, Sage.* New York, NY: Harmony Books. 2000.

BIBLIOGRAPHY

Bruyere, Rosalyn L. *Wheels of Light: Chakras, Auras, and the Healing Energy of the Body.*
New York, NY: Fireside, 1994. Print

Dale, Cyndi. *New Chakra Healing: The Revolutionary 32-Center Energy System.*
St. Paul, MN: Llewellyn Publications, 1998. Print.

Doi, Hiroshi. *Iyashino Gendai Reiki-ho: Modern Reiki Method for Healing.*
Coquitlam, British Columbia: Fraser Journal Publishing, 2000. Print.

Eden, Donna. *Energy Medicine: Balancing Your Body's Energies for Optimal Health, Joy and Vitality*
London, England: Penguin Group, 2008. Print.

Emoto, Masaru. *The Hidden Messages in Water.* Trans. David A Thayne.
New York, NY: Beyond Words Publishing, 2004. Print.

Gerber, Richard. *Vibrational Medicine: The #1 Handbook of Subtle-Energy Therapies.* Third Ed.
Rochester, Vermont: Bear & Company, 2001. Print.

Govinda, Kalashatra. *A Handbook of Chakra Healing: Spiritual Practice for Health, Harmony, and Inner Peace.* Old Saybrook, CT: Konecky & Konecky, 2002. Print.

Hart, Francene. *Sacred Geometry of Nature: Journey on the Path of the Divine.*
Rochester, Vermont: Bear & Company, 2017. Print

Judith, Anodea. *Wheels of Life: A User's Guide To The Chakra System.*
Woodbury, MN: Llewellyn Publications, 2010. Print.

Khalsa, Dharma Singh and Cameron Stauth. *Meditation as Medicine: Activate The Power Of Your Natural Force.* New York: Simon & Schuster, Inc. 2001. Print.

Lee, Ilchi. *Healing Chakra: Light to Awaken My Soul.* Sedona, AZ: Healing Society. 2005. Print.

Lubeck, Walter and Frank Arjava Petter and William Lee Rand. *The Spirit of Reiki: The Complete Handbook of the Reiki System.* Twin Lakes, WI: Lotus Press. 2009. Print.

Miller, Jessica A. *Reiki's Birthplace: A Guide To Kurama Mountain.*
Sedona, AZ: Infinite Light Healing Studies Center, Inc. 2006. Print.

Orloff, Judith. *Intuitive Healing: 5 Steps To Physical, Emotional, and Sexual Wellness.*
New York, NY: Random House, Inc. 2000. Print.

Pond, David. *Chakras For Beginners: A Guide to Balancing Your Chakra Energies.*
Woodbury, MN: Llewellyn Publications, 2009. Print.

Rand, William Lee. *Reiki For A New Millennium.* Southfield, MI: Vision Publications, 1998. Print.

Rand, William Lee. *The Healing Touch: First and Second Degree Manual.*
Southfield, MI: Vision Publications, 2005. Print

Stein, Diane. *Essential Reiki: A Complete Guide to an Ancient Healing Art.*
Berkeley, CA: The Crossing Press, 1995. Print

Usui, Mikao and Frank Arjava Petter. *The Original Reiki Handbook of Dr. Mikao Usui.*
Twin Lakes, WI: Lotus Press, 2011. Print.

CPSIA information can be obtained
at www.ICGtesting.com
Printed in the USA
BVHW021040250319
543606BV00004B/15/P